CW00494632

Presented by:

_____

To:

_____

Date:

_____

Occasion:

_____

Like a Drop
in the Ocean

Dear Mum,

Happy Birthday

Love,

Paul

25. 6. 2011

"99 Words to Live By"

A series of fine gift books that presents inspirational words by renowned authors and captivating thinkers. Thought-provoking proverbs from many peoples and traditions complete each volume's collection.

"99 Words to Live By" explores topics that have moved and will continue to move people's hearts. Perfect for daily reflection as well as moments of relaxation.

Like a Drop
in the Ocean

99 Sayings
by Mother Teresa

edited by
W. Bader

New City Press
Hyde Park, New York

Published in the United States by New City Press
202 Cardinal Rd., Hyde Park, NY 12538
©2006 New City Press (English translation)

Translated by William Hartnett
from the original German edition
Wie ein Tropfen im Ozean
©1997 Verlag Neue Stadt, Munich.

Cover design by Leandro De Leon

Library of Congress Cataloging-in-Publication Data:

Teresa, Mother, 1910-1997
  [Wie ein Tropfen im Ozean. English]
Like a drop in the ocean: 99 sayings / by Mother
Teresa ; edited by W. Bader.
   p. cm. -- (99 words to live by)
  ISBN-13: 978-1-56548-238-8 (alk. paper)
  ISBN-10: 1-56548-238-7 (alk. paper)
  1. Christian life--Catholic authors. I. Bader, Wolfgang,
1948-. II Title. III. Series.
BX2350.3.T4713 2006
242--dc22   2005026543

Printed in Canada

Gonxha Agnes Bojaxhiu, even though she never bore a child physically, deserves the name by which everyone knows her: Blessed Mother Teresa of Calcutta.

This collection of her sayings reveals the qualities that we treasure in every mother: playfulness, compassion, humility, calmness, evenhandedness, the ability to reprove wrongdoing with firmness and love, the ability to maintain a sense of humor even in the most dire circumstances.

But they also reveal much more. Just as Mother Teresa did things that few others could do, she also said things that only she could say. Each of the sayings in this little book reveals her love, her justice, her charity, her dignity as a woman and as a mother to every person she had met. These words are alive because they come from a person who always listened to the living Word. In them we will certainly find the right phrase for many a situation, both difficult and pleasant. Even more, in them Blessed Mother Teresa remains alive, and through her the Spouse she so loved, and so wants us to love.

Thomas Masters

We know only too well that what we are doing is nothing more than a drop in the ocean. But if the drop were not there, the ocean would be missing something.

It is not what we do that is important, but how much love we put into what we do: we should do small things with great love.

I am only God's pencil,
one that he uses
to sketch
whatever he wants.

In order to give love to anyone, we need to enter into contact with that person. If we are only interested in large numbers, we will get lost in numbers and never be able to encounter a single person with love and attention. I believe in the things that happen person to person. For me each person is Christ and since there is only one Lord, the person that I meet in any given moment, to me, is totally unique.

It is impossible to love two people totally. But you can love all persons in a total way if you love Jesus in them.

For us
no one is too miserable
not to be the image of God.

I do not see
the poor beggar,
I see Jesus
who suffers in the beggar
and says:
*I was hungry
and you gave me food . . .*

People are often ashamed of their misery when in their past life things were going better. Once a man came to us who had previously been well off.

He said: "Mother Teresa, I can't stomach the food that you offer us." "I eat it every day," I replied.

He stared at me in wonder and asked: "Do you really eat this stuff?" "Yes," I answered. "Then I can eat it also," he replied.

The fact that I was eating the food gave him the courage to bear his humiliation. If things had been otherwise, perhaps he would have been left with a bitter feeling inside . . .

In order to be able to understand the poor, we must know what poverty is. Otherwise we will be speaking a language that is too different from theirs.

Everything we do is done for Jesus. Our life has no other goal, no other meaning, and yet, so many are not able to understand this. I am at the service of Jesus twenty-four hours a day. I do every action for him and it is he who gives me the strength to do it. I love him in the poor and I love the poor in him, but it is the Lord who always occupies first place.

Whenever we receive a visitor, I always accompany him or her to the chapel saying as I do: "First let us greet the master of the house. Jesus is here: we work for him; it is to him that we give ourselves — and he strengthens us to live this life with joy."

Without Jesus we could never do all that we do, at least not for an entire lifetime. We could do it for one year, perhaps two, but never forever — all of this, without ever expecting anything in return but the possibility to suffer with the One who has loved us to the point of giving his life for us. Without Jesus our life would be absurd, impossible to understand. Only he gives it a sense.

It wasn't I
who had to find Jesus.
It was Jesus who found me.

Never let your worries grow to such a point that they make you forget the joy of the Risen Christ. All of us long for Paradise, but already now we can be with Jesus and share his joy. This means to love as he loves, help as he helps, give as he gives, serve as he serves, save as he saves.

It means being with him twenty-four hours a day and touching him in his worst appearance.

Every time you hand a cup of water to someone who is thirsty, it is to Jesus that you give it. This seems like such a simple teaching, but upon closer examination it appears to be the most important one.

Every thing is small.
But when we offer it to God,
it becomes infinitely great.

The God that we must proclaim is a living God, the God of love. Words must arise from our hearts that are capable of communicating God's joy to the poor.

We will never know how much good a simple smile can do. A smile is like physical contact: it brings something of God into human existence.

Joy should be a distinctive mark of our existence. A joyful sister is like radiant sunshine for the community. Why has God blessed our work in the slums? Not to reward someone's personal qualities, but because of the joy that the sisters radiate. What would our life be like if we sisters were not joyful? We wouldn't be able to attract anyone. Imagine a sister walking through the slums wearing a sad expression and dragging her feet: she wouldn't do any good for the people who live there; on the contrary, she would only increase their sorrow. Joy is contagious and this is why we must always be joyful when we approach a poor person.

When you laugh,
I am able to hear
the music of your smile.

(To her novices)

Joy sprays from your eyes,
from your face
and your every movement.
You cannot suffocate joy,
because it is just pushing
to get out.
When others see
the joy in your eyes,
they know
that they are children of God.

We always need to have a smile on our lips — for every child that we help, for every person that we assist or take care of. It would be a grave mistake if we were only concerned with administering medication. We must give our heart.

When we take care of a person who is sick or poor we touch the suffering body of Christ.

This contact makes us forget our natural reluctance. We must look at these persons with the deep conviction of seeing Christ in them. In these wasting bodies and filthy clothes is hidden the most beautiful of the sons of men. We would need to have the hands of Christ in order to be able to touch these bodies marked with sorrow and pain.

The certainty
that in the leper
I am touching the Christ
gives me the courage
I would not otherwise possess.

No matter how useful and necessary our work might be, it will only be a service occupation if it is not intermingled with suffering. Our work must be Christ's work. He has redeemed us taking our fate upon himself, our mortality, our dying.

If we are to be welcomed
by the poor,
we must live like them.
Poverty is our talent.
We do not endure suffering;
we freely choose it
for love of Jesus
and of the poor.

The *sari* helps the sisters to feel poor among the poor, to identify themselves with the sick, the children, the abandoned elderly. By their manner of dressing, the missionaries of the love of neighbor share in the life of the poor.

There was a very tiny child with us who refused to eat any food. He was sad because his mother had died a short time before. So I looked for a sister that resembled his mother and I told the sister not to do anything else but play with the boy. And then, after a while, the child began to eat again.

We must be
the living image of Jesus
for the children of the slums,
Jesus, who was
the friend of children.

Some time ago I met a small boy on the street. I could see in his face how hungry he was. Who knows how many days it had been since he had eaten? I offered him a piece of bread, and he slowly began tasting it piece by piece. I encouraged him saying, "Eat! Go on, eat it!" Then he looked at me with eyes opened wide and said, "But I'm afraid to eat this bread. I'm afraid that as soon as I finish it I will be hungry again."

Poverty
was not created by God.
We produced it ourselves
— you and I —
with our egoism.

The poor are those who know physical and spiritual privations.
The poor are the hungry, the thirsty . . .
The poor are those without a country, uprooted, the sick and the handicapped . . .
The poor are the lonely people . . .
The poor are the ignorant and the doubtful . . .
The poor are the afflicted.
The poor are the derelicts.
The poor are the angry, the sinners, the jeerers . . .
The poor are the undesired, the outcasts of society.
The poor are we ourselves in some way.

It is more difficult
to fight poverty
in a rich country
than in a poor one.

*(Mother Teresa at the opening
of the Missionaries' third house
for homeless people in London)*

If there were poor
on the moon,
we would have
to go there too.

In Melbourne I went to visit a man who was totally abandoned. His room was in a pitiful state. I wanted to tidy up. "I am fine the way I am," he said, trying to send me away. Finally, though, he allowed me to put the place in order.

Inside that room there was a beautiful lamp all covered with years of dust. "Why don't you light this lamp?" I asked. "Why should I," he replied. "No one ever comes to visit me." "Would you light the lamp if the sisters came to visit you?" I asked. "Yes," he replied. "I would light the lamp if I could hear the sound of someone's voice speaking to me." The following day he sent me this message: "Tell my friend that the light she lit in my life continues to shine."

You can find Calcutta
anywhere in the world.
You only need two eyes to see.
Everywhere in the world
there are people
that are not loved,
people that are not wanted
nor desired,
people that no one will help,
people that are pushed away
or forgotten.
And this is
the greatest poverty.

There is a therapy
or medication
for every sickness,
but not for loneliness,
not for the people
that no one wants.
This is the leprosy
of the West.

I believe that the rich
are poorer than the poor,
because they are
often unhappy.
The more they have,
the more they want.
But not everyone
is like this . . .

It is difficult to fight poverty,
but satisfying the hunger
for bread is easier
than satisfying
the hunger for love.

The worst evil
is the lack of love
for our neighbor.
The greatest evil
is the terrible indifference
towards the people
around us,
towards the outcasts,
the exploited — all those
that have been afflicted
with poverty and sickness.

Over the years
I have become
more and more convinced
that the worst torment
for any human being
is the feeling
of abandonment.

One day I was walking with one of the sisters through the streets of London. A boy caught our attention who had obviously run away from home. I turned to him and said, "Wouldn't it be better for you to return home?" He replied saying, "My mother doesn't want me because my hair is too long. When I go home she doesn't want me." We continued on our way and as we turned a corner we found the boy lying on the sidewalk. He had taken an overdose. We immediately rushed him to the hospital. I thought to myself, "The mother of this boy might do anything she could for the poor in India, but she has no love for her own son." This is what wounds the heart of Jesus most. How can we love the poor if we don't first love our own children?

AIDS is not
a punishment from God.
When we get sick,
we do not acquire any fault.
One of our own sisters
got AIDS from
an infected syringe.
She died slowly.
We are not to express
judgments.

Abortion is terrible
primarily because with it
a mother kills
both life and love:
the life of a child
and the conscience
of a mother.

Children are the most
beautiful gift of God.
Every child has the right
to come into this world
whether or not it is wanted.

Being unwanted
is the worst plight that can
befall a person.
The only cure
is hands that are willing
and ready to serve,
and hearts
that never stop loving.

Be a living sign of God's goodness: goodness in your eyes, goodness on your face, goodness in your smile, goodness in your friendly greeting.

Inside the slums let us be a luminous sign of God's goodness for the poor. Always offer your joyful smile to the children, the poor, to all those who suffer.

Do not offer your help and concern only: give them your heart!

Love each other
as Jesus has loved us.
He has given nothing less
than his life for us.
Therefore, we must give
what is most precious in us.

Jesus asked us
to love each other
as the Father has loved Him.
And how has He loved Him?
By asking Him to die for us.

Love each other . . .
If we are not able
to accept this commandment,
the entire Church of Christ
will fall in on itself.

Works of love for our neighbor are nothing but the outpouring of the love of God that is in us. The more one is close to God, the more one loves one's neighbor.

When we love each other — bringing into our homes the peace, the joy and the presence of the Lord — we can conquer every evil in the world.

Love is a ripe fruit
in all seasons,
and it is
within everyone's reach.

Those who sow love
must be able
to wait for the harvest.

Love's garment has a hem that reaches into the dust, and brushes it away. Therefore, it can sweep away the dirt of streets and villages. It can and it must.

If we truly want to love, we must give until it hurts. Only in this way will we be free of our selves and worthy of others' trust.

Not long ago our kindergarten ran out of sugar. A four-year-old boy heard us talking about it and when he returned home that day he said to his parents, "For three days I am not going to eat any sugar because I want to save it and give it to Mother Teresa." Three days later, he came in with his mother, and gave me the sugar. This little boy could hardly pronounce my name, but he taught me the greatest love. It doesn't matter how much we give, but that we do it with love. That small boy gave until it hurt.

Love cannot stay buried in the heart. No one lights a lamp and then puts it under a bushel basket; instead we put it on a lamp stand so that it can illuminate the whole house.

A few weeks ago a young married couple came to me with a large sum of money for the poor. In Calcutta there are many unfortunates to look after, and every day we feed over nine hundred people.

I asked the couple where they had found so much money. The answer was that they had just been married and had decided together not to spend it on wedding clothes. They wanted to begin their life together with an act of love for others.

This is how the tender love of God reaches people.

What I do others cannot do, and what others do I cannot do. But we all do what God has established for us. It's just that at times we forget this and begin watching what others are doing, and wishing that we could do something different.

Why doesn't God prevent us from doing evil? It is because he did not create people to be like robots, but to be like him, in his image and likeness—that is, as people who are free. When we love others with every fiber of our being, we like them to respond to our love freely.

God loves us in an indescribable way and he leaves us with the freedom of choice, a radical choice: He leaves us free to love, or to refuse love, to irradiate something of the wonderful communion that there is in Christ, or to distance ourselves from it causing others to lose the thirst for the living God also. God leaves us to choose freely; yet in spite of this, he does not leave us all alone nor does he remain inactive. He suffers with us.

Suffering, shared with Christ, is a wonderful gift. It is a sign of his love. How great is God's goodness that it offers us so much suffering and so much love! This gives me joy and strength. Your life full of self-denial helps me. Your prayer and suffering are the chalice into which we can pour the suffering of the people that we meet in the course of our mission. Therefore, you are all as indispensable as we are. Together with you we can do all things in him that is our strength.

(Mother Teresa to collaborators unable to perform physical actions because of their illness)

Whenever suffering comes to us, let us welcome it with a smile. Herein lies the greatest gift of God being able to welcome everything with a smile, everything that He gives us, everything that he asks of us.

True sanctity lies in doing the will of God with a smile. At times, it turns out that it is hard for me to smile at Jesus, because He really asks so much of me.

At first I thought
I had to convert.
Then I learned that my task
is to love.
And love converts
when it wants.

Let us not look for great enterprises. The important thing is that we give of ourselves. Only love counts in anything that we do. Our sisters do little things: they help small children, visit the lonely, the sick and the needy. When they tell me that our sisters are only doing ordinary things my response is that even if they help only one person, that is already great. Jesus would have died for only one person.

Let us be faithful in the little things; this is our strength. For God nothing is too small.

Mary is the cause of our joy because she gave Jesus to us. We can also become the cause of joy for others by giving Jesus to them. Now more than ever, people are hungry for Jesus. He is the only solution if we really want to bring peace to our world.

Mary:
God's most beautiful gift
to the human race.

I am forced to bear the burden of fame, but the benefit that I derive from this is only for the love of Jesus. Whenever they talk about me on the television or in the newspapers they talk about the poor, making people interested in them. Therefore, it is worthwhile for me to take on this burden.

Speaking in public in front of many people is a torture for me.

It is easier for me to bathe a leper than to answer a journalist's questions.

An American journalist once told Mother Teresa, "I wouldn't do what you are doing for a million dollars." And Mother Teresa answered, "Neither would I."

Nothing of what we say
is important,
only what God says
through us.

Words that do not carry the light of Christ increase the darkness around us.

Always write the truth and nothing but the truth. Truth is whatever Jesus says. Don't just write in order to cause a stir or provoke a reaction. People will end up becoming what they read! Someone once said, "Tell me what you read and I'll tell you who you are." Those who have received power and talent from God have to use them solely for giving Him honor and praise, and for the good of others.

A journalist once asked Mother Teresa, "What do you think should change in the Church?" She replied, "You and I."

What has happened during Church history will pass away. For Christ, the Church is always the same: today, yesterday and forever.

The apostles experienced fear and discouragement, failure and infidelity; and yet, Christ did not reprimand them but simply told them, *"Have faith! Why are you afraid?"*

I would like us to love as He has loved.

People are not looking for your talents; they are searching for God who is in you. Lead them to him, not to yourselves. When you do not lead others to God you are seeking yourselves and you are loved for yourselves, not because you recall Jesus.

*(Mother Teresa
to a group of priests)*

Anyone
who is filled with joy
preaches
without preaching.

Trees, flowers, and grass
grow in silence.
Stars, sun, and moon
move in silence.
Silence gives
a new vision of things.

Prayer
gives us a pure heart,
and a pure heart
is able to look at God.

For me, peace means being one with God. Christ is the peace of God. My heart opens to him the more I realize that he is peace. For Christ, all people are brothers and sisters. Once we begin to follow him, there will no longer be wars. Wherever there is anyone who takes Jesus seriously, there you will find peace.

Just think:
the Creator of the Universe
has found time for us,
time for us,
his small creatures.

Life is vital.
We need to protect it.

The fruit of silence
is prayer.
The fruit of prayer
is faith.
The fruit of faith
is love.
The fruit of love
is service.
The fruit of service
is peace.

Peace springs forth from those who sow love and allow it to mature until it bears fruit. We have been made to love and be loved.

We must have the eyes of faith in order to recognize in the failing bodies and filthy clothes the countenance of Christ, the most beautiful of the sons of men.

We must have the hands of Christ in order to assist these bodies marked by suffering.

We must touch these bodies of the poor and languishing with the same love, the same respect, and the same faith with which a priest elevates a consecrated Host.

When we pray, we become a ray of the sunshine of God's love: at home, in the place we are working, for the entire world.

How great is the love of Jesus that he shows to us in the Eucharist! He becomes bread of life in order to satisfy our hunger for love. He makes himself hungry, so that we can satisfy the hunger of his love for us.

We begin our day by trying to see Christ beneath the species of bread and wine. We carry on throughout the day by trying to meet him in the emaciated bodies of our poor.

The wellspring from which you drink must be very deep. In this way, those whom you love will sooner or later discover its source.

Let us leave our future plans to God, since tomorrow has not yet come. We only have today to help people to discover God, to love him, and to serve him.

Christ told us not to worry about tomorrow because it is in the hands of God. Therefore, the future does not worry us. Jesus is always the same — yesterday, today, and tomorrow. He is always himself, and everything depends on him.

Jesus is
the word
that I want to say,
the truth
that I want to proclaim,
the life
that I want to follow,
the light
that I want to enkindle,
the love
that I want to irradiate,
the happiness
that I want to give,
the peace
that I want to bring.

Jesus is the hungry person that I want to feed. Jesus is the thirsty person whose thirst I want to quench. Jesus is the homeless person that I want to welcome in. Jesus is the sick person that I want to care for. Jesus is the lonely person that I want to love. Jesus is the undesired person that I want to accept. Jesus is the abandoned child that I want to take in. Jesus is the drug addict whose friend I want to be. Jesus is the prostitute that I want to steal from harm's way. Jesus is the elderly person that I want to take care of.

We cannot see Christ. Therefore we cannot tell him how much we love him. But we see our neighbor. We can do for him or her what we would do for Christ if we could see him.

For me, Jesus is my God, my spouse, my life, my only love, my all-in-all, my One-and-all. I love him with all my heart, with my entire being.

I gave everything to Jesus, even my sins. And he took me as his spouse with tenderness and love. Now and for all of my life I am the spouse of my crucified spouse.

Many people die exactly as they lived. Death is nothing more than the continuation of life, its completion. This life is not the end; those who believe this are really afraid of death. If people could convince themselves that death means returning to God's house, they would not be afraid.

A question put
to Mother Teresa:
"Do you fear death?"
Her answer:
"Why?"

Jesus gives us the gift of his friendship for our entire life and he wraps us in the tenderness of his love. It is so wonderful that God loves us *tenderly*. Our courage and joy derive from the certainty that nothing can ever separate us from the love of Christ.

Only in Paradise will we realize that we owe a debt to the poor, because they have helped us to love God better.

Organizations and Corporations

This title is available at special quantity discounts for bulk purchases for sales promotions, premiums, or fundraising.
For information call or write:

New City Press, Marketing Dept.
202 Cardinal Rd.
Hyde Park, NY 12538.
Tel: 1-800-462-5980;
1-845-229-0335
Fax: 1-845-229-0351
info@newcitypress.com